THE ASTROLOGY BOOK OF DAYS

An Illustrated Perpetual Calendar

by Susan Miller
Illustrated by Linda DeVito Soltis

Warner ⓦ Treasures
Published by Warner Books
A Time Warner Company

To my mother, Erika Redl Trentacoste, who opened my eyes to the planets, the moon, and the stars, and in so doing, to the sweetness and beauty that this universe provides.

Special thanks to my publisher, editor, and longtime friend Jackie Merri Meyer for the steadfast faith and support she has shown me.

Special thanks, too, to Sarah Brennan-Green and Robert Britton, research librarians who advised me about the various sources available for discovering the birthdays of the famous people found in this book. Their helpfulness and good spirit was much appreciated.

Text copyright © 1996 by Susan Miller

Illustrations copyright © 1996 by Linda DeVito Soltis

Book design by Lisa C. McGarry

Warner Treasures is a trademark of Warner Books, Inc.
1271 Avenue of the Americas,
New York, NY 10020

 A Time Warner Company

Printed in Singapore

First Printing: September 1996

10 9 8 7 6 5 4 3 2 1

ISBN: 0-446-91131-3

Keep in touch with Susan Miller all year long on her web site at
http://pathfinder.com/twep/astrology

THIS BOOK BELONGS TO

Edmund

CAPRICORN

JANUARY

1
New Year's Day

Paul Revere, American patriot and silversmith
Alfred Stieglitz, photographer
Frank Langella, actor

2

Isaac Asimov, writer
Christy Turlington, model
Roger Miller, singer

3

Mel Gibson, actor
Bobby Hull, hockey player
Jim Everett, football player

4

Michael Stipe, R.E.M. singer
Jean Dixon, astrologer
Louis Braille, inventor of Braille system

5

Diane Keaton, actress
Robert Duvall, actor
Alvin Ailey, choreographer

6

Carl Sandburg, poet
Nancy Lopez, golfer
John Singleton, filmmaker

7

Nicholas Cage, actor
Katie Couric, TV journalist
Kenny Loggins, singer and songwriter

8

Elvis Presley, singer
David Bowie, singer
Charles Osgood, TV journalist

9

Joan Baez, singer
Crystal Gayle, singer
Judith Krantz, writer

10

Rod Stewart, singer
Pat Benatar, singer
George Foreman, heavyweight boxing champion

11

Alexander Hamilton, first United States secretary of the treasury
Naomi Judd, singer
Grant Tinker, TV executive

12

John Singer Sargent, artist
Jack London, writer
Kirstie Alley, actress

13

Robert Stack, actor
Julia Louis-Dreyfus, actress
Penelope Ann Miller, actress

14

Albert Schweitzer, physician, philosopher, and African missionary
Andy Rooney, TV journalist
Faye Dunaway, actress

15

Martin Luther King, Jr., civil rights leader
Lloyd Bridges, actor
Molière, playwright

16

Francesco Scavullo, photographer
Kate Moss, model
Debbie Allen, dancer and choreographer

17

James Earl Jones, actor
Muhammad Ali, heavyweight boxing champion
Jim Carrey, actor

18

Kevin Costner, actor
Cary Grant, actor
Oliver Hardy, comic actor

Aquarius is an analytical, somewhat idiosyncratic sign who likes to experiment and discover things independently. Staunch realists, Aquarians are more intellectual than emotional, even in matters of the heart. The planet Uranus, which governs change, eccentricity, surprise, upheaval, electricity, creativity, and genius, rules this sign of innovation. Symbolized by a water bearer, Aquarius "pours" life-giving energy and knowledge back into the heavens. The realm of Aquarius is the universe and the future. Although its symbol includes water, Aquarius is an air sign, and, like Gemini and Libra, has strong communication skills.

Aquarians have great sensitivity for humanitarian issues and social injustice. At some point in their lives most Aquarians champion at least one cause, whether large or small. They care about issues of global importance, such as the environment. Aquarians help others within the structure of solid organizations, unlike Pisceans, who work on an individual level.

Whatever their cause may be, Aquarians assume leadership roles and lay the groundwork for others to follow, leaving the details to others. This sign excels in politics—more United States presidents have been born under this sign than under any other. Their desire to improve society and their powerful charisma makes Aquarians natural leaders. Their ideal world celebrates friendship and brotherhood. They exhibit fairness in their dealings and treat everyone, regardless of their status, with utmost respect. Aquarians have many friends, but only a few become part of their intimate, inner circle. This aloofness gives Aquarians an aura of mystery, which adds to their allure.

Aquarians don't care about following precedent. They are visionaries with their own approach and a focus straight ahead. Equipped with a "third eye," an ability to see the future, Aquarians are often first to identify important social trends. With this forward-looking quality, they are leaps ahead of the rest of the zodiac in the sphere of technology and science, an area where many Aquarians have made their mark.

If you love an Aquarian, give that person a lot of space. Nothing will drive an Aquarian away faster than feeling hemmed in. Your beloved is highly independent and won't commit easily to a relationship. Although Aquarius is not a particularly cautious sign, every Aquarian values freedom and wants to know everything about their betrothed before saying "I do." But once this happens, the Aquarian is loyal, and your life will be filled with change and unexpected events that will never be boring or routine.

19

Edgar Allan Poe, writer and poet
Janis Joplin, singer and songwriter
Dolly Parton, singer

20
Aquarius

Federico Fellini, filmmaker
David Lynch, filmmaker
Patricia Neal, actress

21

Geena Davis, actress
Placido Domingo, opera singer
Jack Nicklaus, golfer

22

George Balanchine, choreographer
John Hurt, actor
D. W. Griffith, filmmaker

23

Princess Caroline of Monaco
Edouard Manet, artist
Chita Rivera, singer and dancer

24

Mary Lou Retton, Olympic gymnast
John Belushi, actor
Nastassja Kinski, actress

25

Edwin Newman, journalist
Virginia Woolf, writer
W. Somerset Maugham, writer

26

Paul Newman, actor
Wayne Gretzky, hockey player
Eddie van Halen, singer

27

Bridget Fonda, actress
Wolfgang Amadeus Mozart, composer
Lewis Carroll, writer and photographer

28	Mikhail Baryshnikov, dancer Alan Alda, actor Arthur Rubinstein, pianist
29	Oprah Winfrey, TV talk show host and actress Tom Selleck, actor W. C. Fields, comic actor
30	Franklin Delano Roosevelt, 32nd United States president Vanessa Redgrave, actress Gene Hackman, actor
31	Norman Mailer, writer Franz Shubert, composer Carol Channing, actress and singer

GIFT IDEAS FOR
THE AQUARIUS MAN

*Anything electronic (a CD player, computer, video games,
CD-ROM disks, a home fax, a car phone, etc. . . .) • a donation in his name to
a favorite cause • membership to a science museum • dinner at a modern,
trendy restaurant that serves innovative cuisine*

GIFT IDEAS FOR
THE AQUARIUS WOMAN

*Anything electronic (a beeper with voice-mail capability, a video
recorder, a laptop computer, an instant camera, computer software) • an astrology
book (Aquarius rules astrology) • an aromatherapy massage
• a sweater in cobalt blue*

AQUARIUS

FEBRUARY

1

Laura Dern, actress
Clark Gable, actor
Victor Herbert, composer

2

Groundhog Day

James Joyce, writer
Farrah Fawcett, actress
Christie Brinkley, model

3

Gertrude Stein, writer
Morgan Fairchild, actress
Blythe Danner, actress

4

Charles Lindbergh, aviator
Betty Friedan, writer and feminist
Erich Leinsdorf, conductor

5

Barbara Hershey, actress
Henry "Hank" Aaron, baseball player
Arthur Ochs Sulzberger, Sr., publisher of the *New York Times*

6

Babe Ruth, baseball player
Tom Brokaw, TV journalist
Ronald Reagan, 40th United States president

7

Charles Dickens, writer
Gay Talese, writer
Garth Brooks, singer

8

Ted Koppel, TV journalist
James Dean, actor
Jack Lemmon, actor

9

Mia Farrow, actress
Joe Pesci, actor
Gypsy Rose Lee, entertainer

10

Boris Pasternak, writer
Leontyne Price, opera soprano
Mark Spitz, Olympic swimmer

11

Thomas Edison, inventor
Leslie Nielsen, actor
Sheryl Crow, singer

12

Abraham Lincoln, 16th United States president
Charles Darwin, scientist
Arsenio Hall, TV talk show host

13

Stockard Channing, actress
George Segal, actor
Chuck Yeager, pilot

14

Valentine's Day

Molly Ringwald, actress
Gregory Hines, actor and dancer
Jack Benny, entertainer

15

Jane Seymour, actress
Marisa Berenson, actress
Galileo Galilei, astronomer and inventor

16

Edgar Bergen, ventriloquist
John McEnroe, tennis player
Giambattista Bodoni, type designer

17

Michael Jordan, basketball player
Red Barber, sportswriter
Hal Holbrook, actor

18

John Travolta, actor
Yoko Ono, singer and artist
Cybill Shepherd, actress

PISCES

February 19–March 20

"I Believe"

Other signs cannot match the emotional intensity of Pisceans, which is expressed in their large and often beautiful eyes. The symbol of this sign is two fish that swim at once upstream and downstream, representing the Pisces dilemma: whether to go with the current or against it. Pisceans are highly impressionable and easily influenced by the emotions of others. They can assimilate themselves to any situation—or they can simply swim away.

Pisces is a water sign, and still water runs deep. Pisceans have an intuitive, even psychic ability that allows them to know what you wanted to say before you say it. Their highly symbolic dreams are often prophetic. Like Scorpios and Cancers, Pisceans can read body language extremely well. A Piscean won't simply take your word for something, but puts faith in your actions and senses the true spirit behind them.

Pisceans need to relieve suffering in others, for they feel others' pain as if it were their own. Send a cry for help, and a Piscean will always answer. Pisceans haven't learned to say "no" and never will. They know that others do not necessarily intend to inflict pain so they can forgive a slight easily. Pisceans believe in fairy tales and happy endings. When reality gets too harsh, this gentle sign retreats into a world of its own creation. While this seems escapist, Pisceans' rich and varied imagination helps them to cope with difficult situations.

Many Pisceans work in the arts or the social sciences where they help people one-on-one. With an acute sensitivity to their environments, they see beauty in things that other signs may overlook, often producing profoundly creative art as a result. Since Pisces rules the domain of nonverbal communication, ballet, poetry, and photography, which rely on symbols and imagery, come under this sign. Pisceans also excel in film, writing, acting, music, social service, psychology, and charity work.

Money does not motivate Pisceans, for this sign is not materialistic. A Piscean who won the lottery would build a hospital or start a foundation, rather than keep the money for personal use. As the last sign of the zodiac, Pisces encompasses the qualities of all the earlier signs before it, so Pisceans are considered to have well-developed personalities. Philosophy, religion, and spirituality are their domain, and your discussions with them on these topics will be deep and meaningful. No one will understand you quite as well as a Piscean, who listens not only with their ears but with their whole heart.

A Piscean will not enter a relationship quickly but will test the other person's loyalty and devotion first, after which a flood of emotion will flow toward their beloved. Pisceans are visionaries and dreamers who reveal to their loved one the possibilities in life that they never imagined. If you love a Piscean, your life will be filled with magic. Treasure your enchanting Piscean, for you have found a compassionate, imaginative partner who will surround you with endless love.

19
Pisces

Prince Andrew of England, Duke of York
Justine Bateman, actress
Nicolaus Copernicus, astronomer

20

Cindy Crawford, model
Ansel Adams, photographer
Robert Altman, filmmaker

21

W. H. Auden, poet
Erma Bombeck, writer
Billy Baldwin, actor

22

Drew Barrymore, actress
Frédéric Chopin, composer
Edna St. Vincent Millay, poet

23

Peter Fonda, actor
Elston Howard, baseball player
W.E.B. DuBois, social reformer and writer

24

Winslow Homer, artist
Paula Zahn, TV journalist
Wilhelm Grimm, fairy-tale writer

25

Bobby Riggs, tennis player
Pierre-Auguste Renoir, artist
Sally Jessy Raphaël, TV talk show host

26

Michael Bolton, singer
Jackie Gleason, comedian
Victor Hugo, writer

27

Elizabeth Taylor, actress
Joanne Woodward, actress
Ralph Nader, consumer activist

28

29

GIFT IDEAS FOR
THE PISCES MAN

A signed, fine-art photograph • tickets to a concert or film opening • membership to a T'ai Chi studio • scuba-diving lessons • a saltwater aquarium with exotic, brilliantly colored fish • an adjustable shower • an important objet d'art from Asia

GIFT IDEAS FOR
THE PISCES WOMAN

A waterproof camera • a short silk negligee in a watery color • her favorite fragrance in bath oils, soaps, and powders • a gift certificate for a body massage • a weekend getaway to a seaside resort • a book of poems • tickets to the ballet • a pair of glamorous evening pumps (Pisces rules the feet)

PISCES

MARCH

1

Chris Webber, basketball player
Harry Belafonte, singer
Ron Howard, filmmaker

2

Tom Wolfe, writer
Lou Reed, singer and songwriter
Jon Bon Jovi, singer

3

Alexander Graham Bell, inventor of the telephone
Jackie Joyner-Kersee, Olympic track athlete
Jean Harlow, actress

4

Ray "Boom Boom" Mancini, boxer
Antonio Vivaldi, composer
Paula Prentiss, actress

5

Rex Harrison, actor
Giovanni Battista Tiepolo, artist
Nikki Taylor, model

6

Michelangelo Buonarotti, artist
Elizabeth Barrett Browning, poet
Shaquille O'Neal, basketball player

7

Maurice Ravel, composer
Anthony Armstrong-Jones, Lord Snowdon, photographer
Michael Eisner, chairman of the Disney Company

8

Aidan Quinn, actor
Lynn Redgrave, actress
Buck Williams, basketball player

9

Micky Spillane, writer
Bobby Fischer, chess champion
Raul Julia, actor

10

Sharon Stone, actress
Chuck Norris, actor
Prince Edward of England

11

Rupert Murdoch, media magnate
Dorothy Schiff, publisher
Sam Donaldson, TV journalist

12

Liza Minnelli, singer and actress
Andrew Young, civil rights leader and United Nations ambassador
Edward Albee, playwright

13

Percival Lowell, astronomer
Walter H. Annenberg, publisher and philanthropist
Neil Sedaka, singer

14

Albert Einstein, scientist
Michael Caine, actor
Billy Crystal, actor and comedian

15

Andrew Jackson, 7th United States president
Sly Stone, musician
Fabio, model

16

Jerry Lewis, comic actor
James Madison, 4th United States president
Bernardo Bertolucci, filmmaker

17

St. Patrick's Day

Rudolf Nureyev, ballet dancer
Nat "King" Cole, singer and pianist
Kurt Russell, actor

18

Edgar Cayce, psychic
Bonnie Blair, Olympic speed skater
Nikolai Rimsky-Korsakov, composer

Aries, the first sign of the zodiac, signifies birth, renewal, and hope. Symbolized by a ram who climbs to the very top of the mountain, the Arian is full of energy and individuality with a role in life of leadership and achievement. Arians are self-sufficient, with strong self-esteem and a determination to make their mark upon the world. As a fire sign, these creative dreamers are highly entrepreneurial and realize their grand ideas through sheer force of will and enthusiasm. Naturally rebellious against authority, Arians are born leaders who like to be in charge. They don't enjoy following someone else's orders. Though they are not detail-oriented, few can lead or inspire the troops as well as Arians. Their brand of optimism and confidence is contagious.

Mars, which governs warriors and bravery, rules Arians, who love challenges and risks. Arians don't allow pain, whether physical, emotional, or financial, to get in their way. Knock them down and they will come right back up. Their rebellious natures enable them to start new ventures, but sometimes it is innocence rather than bravado that fuels their fearlessness. Arians are in a hurry and can be a bit reckless and impulsive, but they keep their eyes on the road and know exactly where they are headed. Having no patience for subterfuge and valuing honesty, Arians give their opinions quickly, because they see things as either black or white and don't bother to analyze the shades of gray. Although every Aries has a temper, another influence of the sign's ruler, Mars, it doesn't last long. Once Arians express their feelings, they soon put their anger behind them.

Arians excel in any profession that requires strong leadership or strenuous physical effort. They make excellent sales people, because their resilience enables them to withstand rejection. Success in sales requires initiative, of which Arians have an abundance. In fact, many of their qualities are those of the entrepreneur. With strong physical endurance, a professional athletic or military career would suit them well. Since Arians have an affinity to sharp metals, there are many Arian surgeons.

In love, this sign enjoys the thrill of the chase, so keep your Arian guessing about your true feelings, at least for a little while. Don't be neglectful for long, though, because Arians appreciate and need open displays of affection. The Aries mate—male or female—will stay deeply in love as long as their romance is kept vital. Life with an Arian is never dull and is sure to bring its share of roller-coaster rides. But after all, that is what drew you to the Arian in the first place.

19

Bruce Willis, actor
Glenn Close, actress
Wyatt Earp, United States marshall

20

Spike Lee, filmmaker
Holly Hunter, actress
William Hurt, actor

21

Aries

Johann Sebastian Bach, composer
Rosie O'Donnell, actress and comedienne
Gary Oldman, actor

22

William Shatner, actor
Andrew Lloyd Webber, composer
Leonard "Chico" Marx, comic actor

23

Akira Kurosawa, filmmaker
Joan Crawford, actress
Erich Fromm, writer and psychologist

24

Edward Weston, photographer
Bob Mackie, fashion designer
Harry Houdini, magician

25

Sarah Jessica Parker, actress
Elton John, singer and songwriter
Gloria Steinem, writer and feminist

26

Robert Frost, poet
Joseph Campbell, writer
Sandra Day O'Connor, United States Supreme Court justice

27

Mariah Carey, singer
Quentin Tarantino, filmmaker
Edward Steichen, photographer

28	Reba McEntire, singer Dianne Wiest, actress Ken Howard, actor
29	Pearl Bailey, singer and actress Walt Frazier, basketball player Elle Macpherson, model
30	Vincent van Gogh, artist Warren Beatty, actor Eric Clapton, singer and songwriter
31	Leo Buscaglia, writer Albert Gore, Jr., 45th United States vice president Christopher Walken, actor

GIFT IDEAS FOR THE ARIES MAN

A set of carving knives • a Swiss army knife • a dart game • tickets to a boxing match • a new razor (perhaps an old-fashioned one, with a shaving brush) • a warm sweater in bright red (Aries's lucky color) • a distinctive new hat (Aries rules the head) • a hot and spicy dinner

GIFT IDEAS FOR THE ARIES WOMAN

Hair ornaments • hairbrushes from England (an Aries-ruled country) • a gift certificate to a posh hair salon • sky-diving lessons • a silky slip and matching robe in red

ARIES

APRIL

1
April Fool's Day

Ali MacGraw, actress
Debbie Reynolds, actress
Sergei Rachmaninoff, composer

2

Hans Christian Andersen, writer
Alec Guiness, actor
Emmylou Harris, singer and songwriter

3

Alec Baldwin, actor
Marlon Brando, actor
Eddie Murphy, actor and comedian

4

Maya Angelou, poet
Robert Downey, Jr., actor
Muddy Waters, blues musician

5

Bette Davis, actress
Spencer Tracy, actor
Gregory Peck, actor

6

John Sculley, CEO of Apple Computer
André Previn, conductor
Marilu Henner, actress

7

Francis Ford Coppola, filmmaker
James Garner, actor
William Wordsworth, poet

8

Betty Ford, First Lady
Jacques Brel, singer
Julian Lennon, singer and songwriter

9

Dennis Quaid, actor
Paulina Porizkova, model
Hugh Hefner, founder of *Playboy*

APRIL

10

Joseph Pulitzer, journalist
Matthew Perry, United States Navy admiral
William Bramwell Booth, founder of Salvation Army

11

Oleg Cassini, fashion designer
Joel Grey, actor and singer
Nicholas Brady, United States secretary of the treasury

12

David Letterman, TV talk show host
Scott Turow, writer
Shannen Doherty, actress

13

Thomas Jefferson, 3rd United States president
Samuel Beckett, playwright
F. W. Woolworth, founder of Woolworth stores

14

Emma Thompson, actress
Rod Steiger, actor
John Gielgud, actor

15

Leonardo da Vinci, artist
Henry James, writer
Jeffrey Archer, writer

16

Kareem Abdul-Jabbar, basketball player
Ellen Barkin, actress
Charlie Chaplin, actor

17

J. P. Morgan, financier
Harry Reasoner, TV journalist
Thornton Wilder, writer

18

Clarence Darrow, lawyer
Leopold Stokowski, conductor
Rick Moranis, actor

TAURUS

April 20–May 20
"I Have"

Taurus, symbolized by the bull, is a strong, determined, steady, reliable, patient, and earthy sign. One thing is for sure: You can count on Taureans. They are so stable that getting them to change their minds is like trying to move a mountain. Since Taureans make decisions slowly and deliberately, it is wise to be part of their thinking process early if you want your point of view considered. Otherwise it will be too late to have any influence on them.

Ruled by Venus, Taurus is one of the most sensuous signs in the zodiac. Taureans love comfortable surroundings, fine food (especially chocolate), and good living. Unlike Arians, who go after what they want directly, Taureans use charm and magnetism to get others to come to *them*. While Taureans seem calm, it is wise not to push them too much. Although it takes a lot to get these bulls angry, their tempers can go out of control, and they will stampede anything and everything in their path.

Taurus rules the throat, and many in this sign have distinctive voices or are good singers. Because of their rulership by Venus, and their refined taste, Taureans excel in the arts. You'll find them working as curators at museums and galleries, or as graphic designers. They are true aesthetes, and their Venus influence inspires them to beautify, so many Taureans work as stylists, makeup artists, jewelers, or florists. Their love of fine food leads some under this sign to become chefs.

Taureans are goal oriented and gifted with the ability to make the dreams of others real. They prefer concrete results to abstract concepts and can effect change in a practical sense, backing up their work with budgets, flow charts, deadlines, and facts. Security-minded Taureans treat others' money with the same caution and respect they do their own, so they do well in occupations like real estate, insurance, and finance. As an earth sign, they make talented architects and engineers.

While Taureans like to save money, they also enjoy acquiring material possessions. They need to be surrounded by beauty, whether manmade or natural. However, it is quality, not quantity that is important to them. Taureans always consider the long-term effect of any action, so while their sensuous natures inspire them to collect things of beauty, their practical sides appreciate their inherent value.

Taureans require emotional security and need a partner who will provide it. In turn, this person will truly listen to you, will offer wise, sound advice, will be loyal forever, and will never let you down.

19

Dudley Moore, actor
Paloma Picasso, jewelry designer
Elliot Ness, FBI agent

20
Taurus

Jessica Lange, actress
Ryan O'Neal, actor
Joan Miró, artist

21

Andie MacDowell, actress and model
Anthony Quinn, actor
Charlotte Brontë, writer

22

Jack Nicholson, actor
Odilon Redon, artist
Aaron Spelling, TV producer

23

William Shakespeare, playwright and poet
Sergei Prokofiev, composer
Vladimir Nabokov, writer

24

Barbra Streisand, singer and actress
Shirley MacLaine, actress
Jean Paul Gaultier, fashion designer

25

Al Pacino, actor
Guglielmo Marconi, inventor of radio and telegraph
Edward R. Murrow, TV journalist

26

I. M. Pei, architect
Eugène Delacroix, artist
Carol Burnett, comedienne

27

Ulysses S. Grant, 18th United States president
Samuel F. B. Morse, inventor of Morse code and artist
Jack Klugman, actor

28	James Monroe, 5th United States president Jay Leno, TV talk show host and comedian Ann-Margret, actress and singer
29	Michelle Pfeiffer, actress Daniel Day-Lewis, actor Jerry Seinfeld, comedian and actor
30	Willie Nelson, singer and songwriter Isiah Thomas, basketball player Alice B. Toklas, writer and companion of Gertrude Stein

GIFT IDEAS FOR
THE TAURUS MAN

A small tree or plant • a trip to a botanical garden
• a deluxe color TV • a comfy chair to watch it in • fine imported
chocolates • dinner in a four-star restaurant

GIFT IDEAS FOR
THE TAURUS WOMAN

Flowers • a beautiful vase to display them in • perfume in a
special bottle • a choker • an elegant scarf • a box of chocolates • clothing in
neutral colors and natural fabrics

TAURUS

MAY

1
Joseph Heller, writer
Jack Paar, TV talk show host
Kate Smith, singer

2
Bing Crosby, singer
Dr. Benjamin Spock, pediatrician
Leslie Gore, singer

3
Doug Henning, magician
Frankie Valli, singer
Sugar Ray Robinson, boxer

4
Audrey Hepburn, actress
Randy Travis, singer
Horace Mann, pioneer in modern public education

5
Tammy Wynette, singer
Tyrone Power, actor
James Beard, chef

6
Sigmund Freud, father of psychoanalysis
Orson Welles, actor and filmmaker
Rudoph Valentino, actor

7
Johannes Brahms, composer
Edwin Land, inventor of the Polaroid Land Camera
Robert Browning, poet

8
Don Rickles, comedian
Melissa Gilbert, actress
Angel Cordero, jockey

9
Billy Joel, singer and songwriter
Mike Wallace, TV journalist
Candice Bergen, actress

10

Linda Evangelista, model
David O. Selznick, filmmaker
Thomas Lipton, founder of Lipton Tea

11

Irving Berlin, songwriter
Salvador Dalí, artist
Martha Graham, dancer and choreographer

12

Katharine Hepburn, actress
Frank Stella, artist
Yogi Berra, baseball player and manager

13

Stevie Wonder, singer and songwriter
Richie Valens, singer and songwriter
Peter Gabriel, singer and songwriter

14

George Lucas, filmaker and special effects innovator
David Byrne, musician
Thomas Gainsborough, artist

15

Richard Avedon, photographer
Jasper Johns, artist
Eddy Arnold, singer

16

Debra Winger, actress
Janet Jackson, singer
Pierce Brosnan, actor

17

Dennis Hopper, actor
Sugar Ray Leonard, boxer
Kathleen Sullivan, TV journalist

18

Pope John Paul II
Bertrand Russell, philosopher
Frank Capra, filmmaker

Duality plays a large role in a Gemini's life. Gemini feel more secure, for instance, when they have two of everything: two jobs, two houses, two children, two best friends—whatever it may be—because they never think in terms of one. Symbolized by a pair of twins who fly through the air, Gemini, it has been said, is always looking for its symbolic twin.

Gemini are generous, quick, alert, funny, and hard to pin down. Just when you think you know where they stand, they change their minds. They enjoy a debate and are always well informed and persuasive on whatever side of an issue they happen to take. They don't have double personalities, but rather it's their analytical nature that leads them to examine both sides of every subject.

Their perpetual curiosity makes them superb journalists. Gemini also excel in sales, publishing, public relations, and occupations that require strong verbal skills. Gemini can talk their way in or out of any situation with charm and grace. Gemini rules travel, especially by air, so this sign does well in transportation, postal, and travel fields, all of which require versatility, communication skills, and adaptability.

Gemini need to be well informed, which is why they usually own many books and subscribe to numerous magazines. They are ruled by Mercury, "messenger of the gods," so they are the first to call with a news bulletin. When you receive letters from your Gemini friends, clippings fall out of the envelope, probably on the very subject you needed to know more about. Since Gemini are so involved with communication and cannot bear to be out of touch, the worst thing you could say is that you couldn't reach them. A Gemini would never go on a vacation *incommunicado*; that is not this sign's idea of fun!

An already overburdened Gemini who is asked to do one more thing for you will amaze you by handling it flawlessly and with style. Others wonder how Gemini accomplish so much, but it is continual change that refreshes and excites them. Their need for stimulation and for channeling their abundant energy enables Gemini to do more than one thing at a time. They would become bored otherwise, which is one reason they acquire knowledge on a wide range of subjects. It has been said that Gemini ought to make a good living to support their many hobbies and interests.

In love, a Gemini needs to feel a quality of surprise, change, and continued growth from their partner. If you love a Gemini, your years together will be a multifaceted experience. One thing's for certain: It will be life in the fast lane!

19

Grace Jones, actress
Nora Ephron, writer
Jim Lehrer, TV journalist

20

Cher, actress and singer
Honoré de Balzac, novelist
Jimmy Stewart, actor

21
Gemini

Albrecht Dürer, artist
Henri Rousseau, artist
Raymond Burr, actor

22

Arthur Conan Doyle, writer
Naomi Campbell, model
Laurence Olivier, actor

23

Joan Collins, actress
Douglas Fairbanks, Jr., actor
Franz Kline, artist

24

Priscilla Presley, actress
Bob Dylan, singer and songwriter
Patti LaBelle, singer

25

Connie Sellecca, actress
Ralph Waldo Emerson, philosopher and writer
Miles Davis, jazz trumpeter and bandleader

26

John Wayne, actor
Peter Cushing, actor
Al Jolson, singer

27

Lou Gossett, Jr., actor
Vincent Price, actor
Henry Kissinger, United States secretary of state

28	Ian Fleming, writer Gladys Knight, singer Jim Thorpe, Olympic medalist
29	John Fitzgerald Kennedy, 35th United States president Annette Bening, actress Bob Hope, actor and comedian
30	Benny Goodman, clarinetist and bandleader Gale Sayers, football player Mel Blanc, voice of Looney Tunes characters
31	Clint Eastwood, actor Joe Namath, football player Brooke Shields, actress

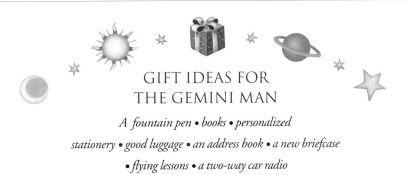

GIFT IDEAS FOR
THE GEMINI MAN

A fountain pen • books • personalized

stationery • good luggage • an address book • a new briefcase

• flying lessons • a two-way car radio

GIFT IDEAS FOR
THE GEMINI WOMAN

Personalized stationery • a cellular phone • a fax/modem

• fashionable jewelry (Gemini rules accessories) • a leather belt with a special buckle

• good luggage • airline tickets for two

GEMINI

JUNE

1
Marilyn Monroe, actress
Andy Griffith, actor
Nelson Riddle, bandleader

2
Thomas Hardy, writer
Dana Carvey, actor and comedian
Stacy Keach, actor

3
Tony Curtis, actor
Josephine Baker, dancer and actress
Raoul Dufy, artist

4
Bruce Dern, actor
Robert Merrill, opera singer
Dennis Weaver, actor

5
Bill Moyers, TV journalist
John Maynard Keynes, economist
Ken Follett, writer

6
Thomas Mann, writer
Diego Velazquez, artist
Nathan Hale, American patriot

7
⚤, formerly known as Prince, singer and songwriter
Jessica Tandy, actress
Paul Gauguin, painter

8
Frank Lloyd Wright, architect
Robert Schumann, composer
Joan Rivers, comedian

9
Johnny Depp, actor
Michael J. Fox, actor
Cole Porter, songwriter

10

Judy Garland, actress and singer
Gustave Courbet, artist
Maurice Sendak, children's book writer and illustrator

11

Jacques-Yves Cousteau, oceanographer
Joe Montana, football player
Gene Wilder, actor

12

George Bush, 41st United States president
Anne Frank, diarist
David Rockefeller, banker

13

William Butler Yeats, poet
Tim Allen, actor and comedian
Ally Sheedy, actress

14
Flag Day

Margaret Bourke-White, photographer
Harriet Beecher Stowe, writer
Eric Heiden, Olympic speed skater

15

James Belushi, actor
Saul Steinberg, artist
Helen Hunt, actress

16

Joyce Carol Oates, writer
Stan Laurel, comic actor
Erich Segal, writer

17

Igor Stravinsky, composer
M. C. Escher, artist
Dan Jansen, Olympic speed skater

18

Isabella Rossellini, actress
Paul McCartney, singer and songwriter
E. G. Marshall, actor

CANCER

June 21–July 22
"I Feel"

Cancer's home is their castle, and no matter how modest or luxurious the abode, it is where their heart lies. The symbol for Cancer is the crab, which is fitting, because the little crab wears its home on its back and takes home wherever it goes. Cancers can easily begin to feel defenseless without the energy and life-giving strength their home provides. Cancers would rather own property than rent or live out of a suitcase, and they always prefer to live near water, because it has a rejuvenating effect on them.

A Cancer has a big heart and cares about the feelings of others. Both the males and females of the sign have a well-known need to nurture. Like Pisceans and Scorpios, they excel at reading body language and know instantly if a person's words and actions are in conflict. Their instinct is always accurate, and they only go off track when they ignore their intuition. Cancers respond quickly to a plea for help. They will listen to you attentively and offer sound advice. However, Cancers rarely relate their innermost feelings. They are intensely private, and they open up only after they feel safe with you. If they aren't ready to talk about something, they will retreat into their shells. Nothing can be done about this until they decide to come out, so it is best to be patient. This sign needs time to retreat and meditate alone.

When it comes to money, Cancers spend carefully and look for the best prices. They dislike wastefulness, and they hold on to their purchases for a long time. Since Cancer has rulership over food, this sign likes to have an abundance of groceries on hand, just in case—often shopping with coupons, counting their change, and checking receipts for errors. Don't tease them about this habit, because it is one way Cancers eventually amass wealth.

Cancers excel in professions that require nurturing, such as nursing, child care, or teaching. Food-related careers, like a chef, restaurateur, or owner of a gourmet shop also suit them well. The hotel industry is ideal for a Cancer because it is the ultimate in nurturing, providing a home away from home for the weary traveler.

Cancers can be moody, which is an influence of their ruler, the Moon. This moodiness reflects the depth of their feelings and their synchronization with nature. One moment they may be light and carefree, and the next they are worried about something. Since their emotions change so swiftly, don't despair if you are faced with a grumpy one. Cancers soon bounce back to their bright, buoyant selves.

Cancers are loyal partners, and family is a priority for them. They are wonderfully playful and will joyfully read bedtime stories or crawl around on the floor with their children. Few will love you with the depth and passion of a Cancer. With the flow of the tides, and the change of the seasons, your life together will be centered around a solid and warm home life.

19

Kathleen Turner, actress
Paula Abdul, singer and dancer
Lou Gehrig, baseball player

20

Nicole Kidman, actress
Errol Flynn, actor
Danny Aiello, actor

21

Cancer

Juliette Lewis, actress
Norman Cousins, publisher and writer, *Saturday Review*
Mariette Hartley, actress

22

Meryl Streep, actress
Bill Blass, fashion designer
Kris Kristofferson, singer and actor

23

Bob Fosse, choreographer and filmmaker
David Ogilvy, advertising executive
Wilma Rudolph, Olympic runner

24

Fred Hoyle, astrophysicist and astronomer
Jack Dempsey, heavyweight boxing champion
Michele Lee, actress

25

George Orwell, writer
Carly Simon, singer and songwriter
Sidney Lumet, filmmaker

26

Pearl S. Buck, writer
Charlotte Zolotow, children's book writer
Greg LeMond, cycling champion

27

Helen Keller, educator and writer
H. Ross Perot, entrepreneur
Anna Moffo, opera singer

28

Kathy Bates, actress
Mel Brooks, comedian and movie director
John Cusak, actor

29

Robert Evans, producer
Claude Montana, fashion designer
George Washington Goethals, army officer and engineer

30

Lena Horne, actress and singer
Buddy Rich, musician
Susan Hayward, actress

GIFT IDEAS FOR
THE CANCER MAN

*A deluxe photo album • a handsome desk accessory • something for
his boat (many Cancers love to sail) • a framed print of an antique vessel • a box of home-
baked cookies in an antique tin • a meal lovingly prepared by you*

GIFT IDEAS FOR
THE CANCER WOMAN

*Cultured pearls • antique jewelry • clothing in soft, silky fabrics in smoky
grays and blues • something unique for the kitchen • a new cookbook • gourmet cooking lessons
• a shimmery satin negligee in white • her favorite perfume*

CANCER

JULY

1

Diana Spencer, Princess of Wales
Dan Aykroyd, actor
Deborah Harry, singer

2

Hermann Hesse, writer
Cheryl Ladd, actress
Jerry Hall, model

3

Tom Cruise, actor
Tom Stoppard, playwright
Ken Russell, director

4

Gina Lollobrigida, actress
Geraldo Rivera, TV talk show host
Ann Landers and Abigail van Buren, advice columnists

Independence Day

5

Jean Cocteau, artist and filmmaker
Phineas T. Barnum, circus promoter
Huey Lewis, singer

6

Sylvester Stallone, actor
Merv Griffin, producer
Ned Beatty, actor

7

Marc Chagall, artist
Gustav Mahler, composer
Ringo Starr, Beatles drummer

8

Kevin Bacon, actor
Angelica Huston, actress
Philip Johnson, architect

9

Tom Hanks, actor
Brian Dennehy, actor
Jimmy Smits, actor

10

Marcel Proust, writer
James Abbott MacNeill Whistler, artist
Jake La Motta, middleweight boxing champion

11

Georgio Armani, fashion designer
Kristi Yamaguchi, Olympic ice skater
John Quincy Adams, 2nd United States president

12

Henry David Thoreau, writer
George Eastman, founder of Eastman Kodak
Bill Cosby, actor and comedian

13

Harrison Ford, actor
Kenneth Clark, historian and writer
Patrick Stewart, actor

14

Ingmar Bergman, filmmaker
Woody Guthrie, folk singer
Isaac Bashevis Singer, writer

15

Rembrandt van Rijn, artist
Linda Ronstadt, singer
Brian Austin Green, actor

16

Ginger Rogers, dancer and actress
Jean-Baptiste Camille Corot, artist
Orville Redenbacher, popcorn tycoon

17

James Cagney, actor
Donald Sutherland, actor
Phyllis Diller, comedienne

18

Nelson Mandela, president of South Africa
John Glenn, astronaut and United States senator
Hume Cronyn, actor

LEO

July 23–August 22
"I Create"

Leo, symbolized by the majestic lion, is ruled by the Sun, the most brilliant star, center of the universe, and giver of life and strength. Leos are born entertainers, and even if they are not professional performers, there is always a bit of the actor in them. Whether they are at work or play, their flair for the dramatic and their stately, commanding presence makes them memorable.

Like the king of the jungle, Leos have a powerful need for respect and admiration. Leos like to be at the helm, and their confidence and optimism enables them to achieve leadership roles. Many Leos are magnetic political leaders or fine teachers who perform their lessons for their students. They never tire of an audience—as a fire sign Leo burns brighter in the spotlight. Their charisma and strong presence make Leos compelling court attorneys.

Leo rules creativity in all matters, so many Leos have a strong artistic sense. Leos can be found in art-related occupations such as advertising, design, theater, and music. Their superb taste makes them outstanding fashion or jewelry designers. Leos do not hesitate when they make decisions, which encourages others to put their trust in them. Whatever occupation they choose, Leos must have a strong emotional connection to their work.

They are gregarious, generous, warm-hearted, and adore children—either their own or others'—since this sign rules offspring. Like lionesses, Leos are fiercely protective of their "cubs." Leos will sacrifice much for their children, and they usually take an active role in parenting.

You can often spot a Leo by their beautiful, fashionable clothes. A Leo would prefer one designer outfit to a dozen lesser ones; first-class taste won't let Leos settle for second best. They love to dress up in formal attire too, and the male Leo likes to own a tuxedo just in case the need arises. Even though Leos like to be center stage, they are generous to their friends. When a Leo hosts a party, you can expect a well-laid table. If it's a special occasion, the Leo will choose the most elegant spot in town.

Your Leo will love you with a whole heart, which is a big one, and you're sure to have fun together. Leo feels that life is to be enjoyed to the fullest, and there is nothing wrong with that!

19
Edgar Degas, artist
Ilie Nastase, tennis player
Vikki Carr, singer

20
Natalie Wood, actress
Carlos Santana, musician
Edmond Hillary, explorer who first climbed Mt. Everest

21
Robin Williams, actor and comedian
Ernest Hemingway, writer
Janet Reno, United States attorney general

22
Edward Hopper, artist
Danny Glover, actor
Oscar DeLaRenta, fashion designer

23
Leo
Woody Harrelson, actor
Don Drysdale, baseball player
Pee Wee Reese, baseball player

24
Lynda Carter, actress
Amelia Earhart, aviator
Barry Bonds, baseball player

25
Iman, model
Estelle Getty, actress
Nate Thurmond, basketball player

26
George Bernard Shaw, writer
Carl Jung, psychologist
Mick Jagger, Rolling Stones singer and songwriter

27
Peggy Fleming, Olympic ice skater
Norman Lear, TV writer and producer
Keenan Wynn, actor

28

Jacqueline Bouvier Kennedy Onassis, First Lady
Richard Rodgers, composer
Rudy Vallee, entertainer

29

Peter Jennings, TV journalist
Paul Taylor, dancer and choreographer
Dag Hammarskjold, United Nations secretary general

30

Arnold Schwarzenegger, actor
Laurence Fishburne, actor
Casey Stengel, baseball manager

31

Wesley Snipes, actor
Sherry Lansing, movie producer
Geraldine Chaplin, actress

GIFT IDEAS FOR
THE LEO MAN

Tickets to a hot new show • a bottle of fine wine
• an engraved gold pocket watch or lighter • a tin of caviar
• audio equipment for his car or home

GIFT IDEAS FOR
THE LEO WOMAN

Opera tickets • a bottle of good champagne • gold jewelry • a designer
outfit or accessories • a surprise trip to Leo-ruled Rome • a weekend for two in the best hotel
in a big city • an invitation to an art opening • imported jams, teas,
and cookies • a ring of rubies and diamonds

LEO

AUGUST

1
Yves St. Laurent, fashion designer
Herman Melville, writer
Francis Scott Key, composer

2
Carroll O'Connor, actor
Peter O'Toole, actor
Myrna Loy, actress

3
Anne Klein, fashion designer
Tony Bennett, singer
Martin Sheen, actor

4
Percy Bysshe Shelley, poet
Roger Clemens, baseball player
Elizabeth, Queen Mother of England

5
Neil Armstrong, astronaut
Guy de Maupassant, writer
Patrick Ewing, basketball player

6
Lucille Ball, comedienne
Andy Warhol, artist
Alfred Lord Tennyson, poet

7
Mata Hari, spy
Emil Nolde, artist
Don Larsen, baseball player

8
Dustin Hoffman, actor
Dino De Laurentiis, filmmaker
Jerry Tarkanian, basketball coach

9
Melanie Griffith, actress
Whitney Houston, singer
Deion Sanders, football and baseball player

AUGUST

10
Antonio Banderas, actor
Rosanna Arquette, actress
Eddie Fisher, actor

11
Fred Smith, founder of Federal Express
Alex Haley, writer
Hulk Hogan, wrestler

12
Cecil B. DeMille, filmmaker
George Hamilton, actor
John Derek, movie director

13
Alfred Hitchcock, filmmaker
Bert Lahr, actor
Annie Oakley, sharpshooter

14
Earvin "Magic" Johnson, basketball player
Danielle Steel, writer
Steve Martin, actor

15
Napoleon Bonaparte, emperor of France
Julia Child, chef
Gianfranco Ferré, fashion designer

16
Madonna, singer and actress
Kathy Lee Gifford, TV talk show host
Frank Gifford, sportscaster

17
Robert De Niro, actor
Davey Crockett, folk hero
Mae West, actress

18
Robert Redford, actor and movie director
Christian Slater, actor
Patrick Swayze, actor

Virgo, symbolized by the Virgin who carries a sheaf of harvest wheat, is a highly productive sign. Perfectionists at heart, Virgos are never quite satisfied with their work, and they diligently polish it until it gleams.

The Virgin of the symbol refers to their truth-seeking nature and their quest for purity of vision and thought. Virgos see things not as they are, but in the ideal state, as they could be. They are often considered overly critical for this reason, but they can't help calling things as they see them. They suggest improvements simply to be helpful. Their sharp intelligence, earthy practicality, and resourcefulness make them an asset to have around.

Intelligence and verbal skills make Virgos superb writers, research analysts, and communicators. Their ability to make sense out of chaos is one of their primary gifts. In a crisis, Virgos quickly assess the situation and have everything under control and in perfect order. Unlike Leos, who like to lead, shy Virgos are content to do their work from the sidelines. No other astrological sign can match their attention to detail—absolutely nothing escapes their discerning eye. Ask a Virgo a simple question, and the next day you'll get an encyclopedic answer on the subject.

Their meticulousness carries into the physical arena as well. Virgos have superb motor skills, so many Virgos become successful tailors and seamstresses, woodworkers, or illustrators, or become involved in other occupations that require intricate handwork. As this sign rules physical well-being, they make good nutritionists, health care workers, or fitness instructors.

Virgos work hard and often put in extra hours, but they find great satisfaction and enjoyment in what they do. Their steadfast seriousness about their careers always pays off later. Scrupulously honest and ethical, Virgos want to win praise the old-fashioned way: by earning it. They don't succumb to office politics, and they usually avoid them if they can. They exhibit impeccable manners, and fully expect others to do the same.

Virgos take good care of themselves, avoiding junk food and exercising regularly. Though they are worriers, unlike Cancers, Virgos are generally less emotional. They rely on their reasoning ability, earthiness, and a superb talent for knowing where to find answers to enable them to triumph over any obstacles they may face.

If you are in love with a Virgo, you will find that through the years Virgo will remain true to you. Your time together will be enhanced with good discussions and solid communication. Your love will deepen and ripen, like the harvest wheat the Virgo Virgin carries.

19

Bill Clinton, 42nd United States president
Coco Chanel, fashion designer
Malcolm Forbes, publisher

20

Connie Chung, TV journalist
Jacqueline Susann, writer
Robert Plant, Led Zeppelin singer and songwriter

21

Happy Birthday ✱

Count Basie, bandleader
Kenny Rogers, singer
Wilt Chamberlain, basketball player

22

Henri Cartier-Bresson, photographer
Claude Debussy, composer
Norman Schwarzkopf, United States Army general

23

Virgo

Gene Kelly, dancer and actor
Antonia Novello, United States surgeon general
River Phoenix, actor

24

Cal Ripken, Jr., baseball player
Jorge Luis Borges, writer
A. S. Byatt, writer

25

Sean Connery, actor
Claudia Schiffer, model
Althea Gibson, tennis player

26

Peggy Guggenheim, art collector
Guillaume Apollinaire, poet
Benjamin Bradlee, editor of the *Washington Post*

27

Mother Teresa, humanitarian and Nobel Peace Prize recipient
Lyndon B. Johnson, 36th United States president
Man Ray, artist and photographer

28	Jason Priestley, actor Scott Hamilton, Olympic ice skater Ben Gazzara, actor
29	Michael Jackson, singer Ingrid Bergman, actress Robin Leach, TV personality
30	Ted Williams, baseball player Roy Wilkins, NAACP leader Mary Wollstonecraft Shelley, writer
31	Richard Gere, actor William Saroyan, writer Edwin Moses, Olympic track athlete

GIFT IDEAS FOR
THE VIRGO MAN

An electronic diary • software to organize his finances • a laptop computer • woodworking tools • a portable vacuum cleaner for his car • a desk lamp • a weekend at a fitness spa • a subscription to a fruit-of-the-month club

GIFT IDEAS FOR
THE VIRGO WOMAN

A puppy or kitten • a computer • a gift certificate for a manicure and pedicure • a leather agenda • a sewing machine • a needlepoint kit • clothing with detailed work • anything from Virgo-ruled Paris

VIRGO

SEPTEMBER

1

Gloria Estefan, singer and songwriter
Lily Tomlin, comedienne and actress
Ann Richards, Texas governor

2

Keanu Reeves, actor
k.d. lang, singer
Jimmy Connors, tennis player

3

Charlie Sheen, actor
Kitty Carlisle, actress
Valerie Perrine, actress

4

Craig Clairborne, food writer
Tom Watson, golfer
Ione Skye, actress

5

Raquel Welch, actress
Darryl Zanuck, filmmaker
Jack Valenti, Film Association president

6

Jane Curtin, actress
Swoosie Kurtz, actress
Joseph Patrick Kennedy, financier

7

Sonny Rollins, jazz saxophonist
Elia Kazan, stage and film director
Buddy Holly, singer and songwriter

8

Rachel Hunter, model
Peter Sellers, actor
Patsy Cline, singer

9

Michael Keaton, actor
Leo Tolstoy, writer
Otis Redding, singer

10

Karl Lagerfeld, fashion designer
Charles Kuralt, TV journalist
Amy Irving, actress

11

O. Henry, writer
Harry Connick, Jr., singer and pianist
Brian DePalma, filmmaker

12

Jesse Owens, Olympic track and field athlete
Henry Hudson, explorer
Linda Gray, actress

13

Arnold Schoenberg, composer
Jacqueline Bisset, actress
Milton S. Hershey, founder of Hershey's Chocolate

14

Clayton Moore, actor
Mel Torme, singer
Kate Millett, writer

15

Tommy Lee Jones, actor
Oliver Stone, filmmaker
Agatha Christie, writer

16

David Copperfield, magician
Lauren Bacall, actress
J. C. Penney, founder of J. C. Penney department stores

17

Ann Bancroft, actress
William Carlos Williams, poet
John Ritter, actor

18

Greta Garbo, actress
Frankie Avalon, singer
Samuel Johnson, writer

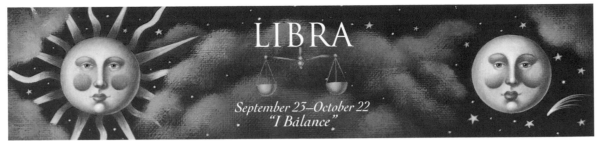

LIBRA

September 23–October 22
"I Balance"

Sweet Libra's charms are irresistible. Ruled by Venus, planet of beauty and love, Libra has a natural affinity for the social graces. Librans love parties and need to interact with others often. Symbolized by a set of scales, Libra seeks proper balance and harmony, but is sometimes frustrated by life's inequities. Even in childhood, it is the Libra who exclaims, "It's not fair!" as if expecting life to be in perfect balance.

Their innate need for equality leads many Librans to enter legal professions. They excel as well in fields where proper proportion or careful negotiation plays a role, such as the arts, music, and social planning. They make talented diplomats, too, relying on their resourcefulness, focus, and the ability to handle delicate situations with finesse.

Librans can be a bit bossy, which often surprises others because it seems so out of character for them. Yet they wield their authority so adeptly and gracefully that they rarely reveal how cleverly they've persuaded you to do exactly what they had in mind. Librans are highly competitive and have strong views on a variety of subjects. An intellectual, analytical air sign like Gemini, Libra also looks at both sides of an issue and weighs its pros and cons before reaching a conclusion. Librans have difficulty choosing one side over another, though, and continue to examine an issue even after they've made a decision.

They collaborate well and prefer teamwork to working in isolation. Libra is the sign of relationships, which is why Librans perform best in the presence of others, who help this sign generate and hone ideas. Librans never take full credit for an endeavor, but carefully acknowledge everyone's contribution. It's no wonder they are popular and have many friends.

Librans do not regard objects of beauty as luxuries, but rather as necessities that provide them with joy and energy. Venus-ruled, this sign in turn rules the decorative arts, which Libra incorporates into everyday life. Items like fresh flowers, fancy chocolate, and elegant clothing often find their way into a Libra home. Librans care about their appearance, another indication of their rulership by Venus, and even with a busy schedule, Librans take the extra time to put their hair into place, adjust a collar, and generally present a finished, well-groomed look to the world.

In love, Libra is quite flirtatious and hard to catch. Like Arians, Librans love the chase, but once they are serious they will expect you, too, to commit. Libra values partnerships, and Librans are usually happier when married and may even feel incomplete otherwise. Since partnering comes so naturally to them, always include their partner's point of view. Marriage for Librans is not only a worthy goal, it is a sacred bond to cherish and uphold throughout their lives.

19

Jeremy Irons, actor
Twiggy, model
Joan Lunden, TV journalist

20

Sophia Loren, actress
Joyce Brothers, psychologist
James Galanos, fashion designer

21

Stephen King, writer
Bill Murray, comic actor
H. G. Wells, writer

22

Franz Liszt, composer
Joan Jett, singer
Shari Belafonte, actress

23

Libra

Bruce Springsteen, singer and songwriter
Julio Iglesias, singer
Ray Charles, singer

24

Jim Henson, creator of the Muppets
F. Scott Fitzgerald, writer
"Mean" Joe Green, football player

25

Michael Douglas, actor
Heather Locklear, actress
Barbara Walters, TV journalist

26

George Raft, actor
George Gershwin, composer
T. S. Eliot, poet and playwright

27

Samuel Adams, Massachusetts governor
Louis Auchincloss, writer
Meat Loaf, singer and songwriter

28	Brigitte Bardot, actress Carrie Otis, model Marcello Mastroianni, actor
29	Gene Autry, singer and actor Bryant Gumbel, TV journalist Jerry Lee Lewis, singer
30	Angie Dickinson, actress Truman Capote, writer Johnny Mathis, singer

GIFT IDEAS FOR
THE LIBRA MAN

A CD player • CDs • fine jewelry with an engraved inscription
• a shearling coat • cologne with a subtle scent • custom-made shirts
• a sterling silver business-card case • a tuxedo

GIFT IDEAS FOR
THE LIBRA WOMAN

A special piece of jewelry (preferably with sapphires) • a bottle of her
favorite perfume • tickets to a concert or the ballet • a framed wall or hand mirror
• an illustrated art book • a day of pampering at a spa • a tiny, elegant evening purse
• a luxurious silk blouse in cream, pale blue, or soft pink

LIBRA

OCTOBER

1
Jimmy Carter, 39th United States president
Walter Matthau, actor
Randy Quaid, actor

2
Sting, singer
Annie Leibovitz, photographer
Donna Karan, fashion designer

3
Gore Vidal, writer
Chubby Checker, songwriter and singer
Dave Winfield, baseball player

4
Susan Sarandon, actress
Anne Rice, writer
Charlton Heston, actor

5
Bob Geldof, musician and activist
Glynis Johns, actress
Louis Lumière, film technology innovator

6
LeCorbusier, architect
George Westinghouse, engineer
Carole Lombard, actress

7
John Mellencamp, singer and songwriter
Desmond Tutu, South African Anglican archbishop
Helen MacInness, writer

8
Sigourney Weaver, actress
Chevy Chase, comic actor
Jesse Jackson, political leader

9
John Lennon, Beatles singer and songwriter
Camille Saint-Saëns, composer
Joe Pepitone, baseball player

10

Giuseppe Verdi, opera composer
Antoine Watteau, artist
Helen Hayes, actress

11

Luke Perry, actor
Eleanor Roosevelt, First Lady
Jerome Robbins, dancer and choreographer

12

Luciano Pavarotti, opera singer
Ronald McNair, astronaut and physicist
Susan Anton, actress

13

Nancy Kerrigan, Olympic skater
Marie Osmond, singer
Margaret Thatcher, prime minister of Great Britain

14

Ralph Lauren, fashion designer
Roger Moore, actor
e. e. cummings, poet

15

Lee Iacocca, CEO of Chrysler Corporation
Penny Marshall, filmmaker
Sarah Ferguson, Duchess of York

16

Tim Robbins, actor
Angela Lansbury, actress
Eugene O'Neill, playwright

17

Arthur Miller, playwright
Rita Hayworth, actress
Margot Kidder, actress

18

George C. Scott, actor
Martina Navratilova, tennis player
Chuck Berry, singer and songwriter

SCORPIO

October 23–November 21
"I Control"

Scorpio is the only sign that has three symbols: the phoenix, the scorpion, and the snake. Each of these, like Scorpio, has the ability to transform itself. The phoenix rises from the ashes, the snake sheds its skin, and the scorpion, who stings in self-defense, perishes in the process. These symbols reinforce the life-death-rebirth cycle associated with this sign. In fact, Scorpios usually have three distinct periods in their lives. Pluto, which governs rebirth, rejuvenation, obsession, power, and unseen phenomena, rules Scorpio and influences its mysterious nature.

Scorpio enjoys the reputation of being the sexiest sign of the zodiac. Confidence is the secret of this allure. A Scorpio won't succumb to flattery or be thrown by criticism. Scorpios decide their worth to the world and are either amused or annoyed when others feel compelled to offer them feedback. Combine this assurance with a certain calmness, and it all adds up to a thrilling, elusive aura.

This sign understands the value of secrecy, and rather than reveal what is going on in their lives, whether in business or personal relationships, Scorpios keep silent. To a Scorpio, the whole world is a potential competitor, and even if not, why reveal anything, anyway? To do so would only stir questions that a Scorpio would rather not answer. Scorpios are not dishonest, but they are loners who are inwardly intense and private about their feelings. Scorpios do not wear their hearts on their sleeve. If you are close to a

Scorpio, you'll need to urge that friend to open up. An intuitive, shrewd, and street-smart sign, Scorpio will soon know your secrets, won't reveal their own, but will, however, make a trustworthy confidant.

Scorpios can become determined, even obsessed, about their goals, and feel frustrated when they can't achieve them. Their resourcefulness makes them superb spies, detectives, investigators and prosecutors. They also work well in positions that require management of big budgets because they are shrewd and ethical, especially with other people's money. Scorpio excels in the field of medicine because of their affinity to unseen entities.

Some people fear Scorpios because of their reputation for vindictiveness. However, Scorpios do not strike unless they face a direct threat. They are intensely loyal and passionate until you betray their trust; then woe upon you, for you will certainly incur their wrath. They will not forget your transgression and will seek revenge, even if it takes years.

Conversely, if you treat a Scorpio well, you will receive more in return than you ever gave, for Scorpio is supremely generous. Scorpios make their mates happy, and give all they have. They are sexy, unforgettable, and magnetic, and will love you with a grand passion. Loving a Scorpio is always a thrilling experience, and it only gets better with time.

19
John Le Carré, writer
Evander Holyfield, heavyweight boxing champion
Peter Max, graphic artist

20
Bela Lugosi, actor
Mickey Mantle, baseball player
Keith Hernandez, baseball player

21
Carrie Fisher, actress
Georg Solti, conductor
Alfred Nobel, inventor of dynamite and founder of the Nobel Prize

22
Catherine Deneuve, actress
Annette Funicello, actress
Brian Boitano, Olympic skater

23
Scorpio
Pele, soccer player
Michael Crichton, writer
Johnny Carson, TV talk show host

24
Kevin Kline, actor
Tito Gobbi, opera singer
Moss Hart, playwright

25
Pablo Picasso, artist
Richard Byrd, polar explorer
Midori, violinist

26
Hillary Rodham Clinton, First Lady
Jaclyn Smith, actress
Domenico Scarlatti, composer

27
Sylvia Plath, poet
Dylan Thomas, poet
John Cleese, comic actor

28

Julia Roberts, actress
Bill Gates, founder of Microsoft Corporation
Dennis Franz, actor

29

Winona Ryder, actress
Richard Dreyfuss, actor
Melba Moore, actress and singer

30

Ezra Pound, poet
Louis Malle, filmmaker
Charles Atlas, bodybuilder

31
Halloween

John Keats, poet
Dan Rather, TV journalist
Jane Pauley, TV journalist

GIFT IDEAS FOR
THE SCORPIO MAN

*Fine leather luggage • a new leather jacket • a high-tech
electronic gadget • an international mystery novel • an umbrella big enough for two
• a set of silk sheets • dinner at a dark and private restaurant*

GIFT IDEAS FOR
THE SCORPIO WOMAN

*A chic designer handbag or wallet • lace or silk lingerie
• a best-selling love story • a belt • a new raincoat • clothing
in natural fabrics in black or burgundy, her lucky colors*

SCORPIO

NOVEMBER

1
Lyle Lovett, singer and songwriter
Stephen Crane, writer
Gary Player, golfer

2
Burt Lancaster, actor
Daniel Boone, folk hero
Dennis Miller, actor

3
Charles Bronson, actor
Roseanne, comedienne and actress
Anna Wintour, editor in chief of *Vogue*

4
Will Rogers, actor
Walter Cronkite, TV journalist
Art Carney, actor

5
Sam Shepard, actor and playwright
Roy Rogers, cowboy actor
Tatum O'Neal, actress

6
Ethan Hawke, actor
Sally Field, actress
Maria Shriver, TV journalist

7
Marie Curie, chemist
Albert Camus, writer
Joan Sutherland, opera singer

8
Bonnie Raitt, singer
Morley Safer, TV journalist
Milton Bradley, founder of Milton Bradley Toy Company

9
Carl Sagan, astronomer and writer
Hedy Lamarr, actress
Tom Weiskopf, golfer

10	Richard Burton, actor
	Roy Scheider, actor
	Martin Luther, religious leader
11 Veteran's Day	Demi Moore, actress
	Fyodor Dostoevsky, writer
	Kurt Vonnegut, Jr., writer
12	Grace Kelly, Princess of Monaco
	Nadia Comaneci, Olympic gymnast
	Elizabeth Cady Stanton, suffragist
13	Whoopi Goldberg, actress
	Robert Lewis Stevenson, writer
	Gary Marshall, writer and movie producer
14	Charles, Prince of Wales
	Claude Monet, artist
	Boutros Boutros-Ghali, United Nations secretary general
15	Sam Waterston, actor
	Georgia O'Keeffe, artist
	Edward Asner, actor
16	Burgess Meredith, actor
	Lisa Bonet, actress
	Paul Hindemith, composer
17	Danny DeVito, actor
	Martin Scorsese, filmmaker
	Isamu Noguchi, sculptor
18	Linda Evans, actress
	Brenda Vaccaro, actress
	Alan B. Shepard, astronaut

SAGITTARIUS

November 22–December 21
"I Think"

Sagittarius is symbolized by a Centaur, a creature that is half man and half horse, who holds a bow and arrow and takes aim. Ruled by Jupiter, the largest planet, also called the lucky planet of optimism, Sagittarius aims high. Blessed with endless energy, this fire sign usually attains goals simply because it fully expects to do so.

Sagittarius rules higher education, and Sagittarians often pursue advanced degrees because they love the process of becoming educated. They are deeply philosophical, so if you are looking for someone to share a discussion on the meaning of life, call a Sagittarian, and be prepared to stay up late. Sagittarians thoroughly discuss any subject at hand. Their interest in investigating theories and their ease in academic environments inspire many Sagittarians to become college professors. Their opposite sign, Gemini, is also intellectual, but focuses instead on everyday events, while Sagittarius examines the larger picture and tries to attain its meaning.

Sagittarians can be brutally honest, no matter how difficult it may be for others to face. You will always get a direct answer from them, even if it isn't one you anticipated. Everyone has been the recipient of a Sagittarius arrow at least once, but their genuine generosity and good intentions are their saving grace, which is why they keep many lifelong friends.

They love to travel to exotic places, so Sagittarians need a mate who can share this passion. They would rather explore a remote part of Africa, the North Pole, or the Far East than see their own state. Since Sagittarians love challenges and are open-minded, they adapt easily to foreign cultures, learning new languages quickly. They do well in occupations that require travel or that require extensive research. Of course, with their ability with languages, Sagittarians make superb translators or interpreters. With a love of physical risks, and a great sense of timing, this sign produces more sports champions than any other sign. They know you have to take chances in order to win.

While Libra is the marriage sign, Sagittarius has been called the bachelor sign. Sagittarians don't have an innate need for this kind of commitment, but can be persuaded to wed the right person. Ruled by expansive Jupiter, Sagittarians need room in a relationship. Sagittarians do love animals, and sometimes a favorite pet forms the object of this sign's affection.

If you fall in love with a Sagittarian you will no doubt enjoy your mate's clever wit and bright optimism. Against all odds, Sagittarians succeed in whatever they set out to do. A constant need for intellectual stimulation makes them hard to keep up with, but you'll find that they are well worth the effort!

19

Jodie Foster, actress
Ted Turner, founder of Turner Broadcasting System
Calvin Klein, fashion designer

20

Robert Fitzgerald Kennedy, United States attorney general and senator
Dick Smothers, comedian
Bo Derek, actress

21

Goldie Hawn, actress
Tina Brown, editor in chief of *The New Yorker*
Marlo Thomas, actress

22
Sagittarius

Jamie Lee Curtis, actress
Rodney Dangerfield, comedian
Billy Jean King, tennis player

23

Boris Karloff, actor
"Harpo" Marx, comic actor
Maxwell Caulfield, actor

24

William F. Buckley, Jr., writer
Geraldine Fitzgerald, actress
Scott Joplin, composer and pianist

25

John F. Kennedy, Jr., lawyer and publisher
Joe Di Maggio, baseball player
John Larroquette, actor

26

Tina Turner, singer
Charles Shultz, cartoonist
Robert Goulet, singer

27

Caroline Kennedy Schlossberg, lawyer and writer
Jimi Hendrix, rock musician
Bruce Lee, actor

28

Ed Harris, actor
William Blake, poet and artist
Alexander Godunov, ballet dancer

29

Louisa May Alcott, writer
Gary Shandling, actor
Suzy Chaffee, Olympic skier

30

Mark Twain, writer
Winston Churchill, prime minister of Great Britain
Dick Clark, TV host and producer

GIFT IDEAS FOR
THE SAGITTARIUS MAN

*A piece of foreign art • tuition for a course he wants
to study • workout clothes • hiking gear • sporting equipment • dinner
at an exotic, foreign restaurant*

GIFT IDEAS FOR
THE SAGITTARIUS WOMAN

*New luggage • horseback riding lessons • a workout video • a clock with
different time zones • membership at a health club • a framed, old map of an exotic
country • a book on a philosophical subject • a series of workshops • computer
software • sporty and informal clothing in rich purple or royal blue*

SAGITTARIUS

DECEMBER

1
Woody Allen, filmmaker and actor
Richard Pryor, actor
Carol Alt, model

2
Georges Seurat, artist
Monica Seles, tennis player
Gianni Versace, fashion designer

3
Daryl Hannah, actress
Joseph Conrad, writer
Katarina Witt, Olympic skater

4
Marisa Tomei, actress
Jeff Bridges, actor
Wassily Kandinsky, artist

5
Walt Disney, creator of Walt Disney Studio
Otto Preminger, filmmaker
Jose Carreras, opera singer

6
Alfred Eisenstadt, photographer
David Brubeck, jazz musician
Ira Gershwin, songwriter

7
Ellen Burstyn, actress
Larry Bird, basketball player
Eli Wallach, actor

8
Kim Basinger, actress
Sinead O'Connor, singer
Jim Morrison, singer

9
Kirk Douglas, actor and writer
John Malkovich, actor
John Milton, poet

10

Emily Dickinson, poet
Kenneth Branagh, actor and filmmaker
Susan Dey, actress

11

Alexander Solzhenitsyn, writer
Rita Moreno, dancer and actress
Susan Seidelman, movie director

12

Frank Sinatra, singer
Bridget Hall, model
Edward G. Robinson, actor

13

Christopher Plummer, actor
Dick van Dyke, actor
Donatello, sculptor

14

Nostradamus, psychic
Patty Duke, actress
Lee Remick, actress

15

Don Johnson, actor
John Paul Getty, industrialist and art collector
Alexandre Eiffel, architect of Eiffel Tower

16

Ludwig van Beethoven, composer
Margaret Meade, anthropologist
Noël Coward, playwright and songwriter

17

William Safire, journalist
Arthur Fiedler, conductor
Willard F. Libby, chemist

18

Brad Pitt, actor
Steven Spielberg, filmmaker
Keith Richards, Rolling Stones guitarist

Capricorn's symbol is a goat ascending a mountain from the depths of the sea. This image captures Capricorns' ambitious nature, especially when it comes to their careers. They are ruled by Saturn, which governs permanence, responsibility, ambition, bones, structure, and foundations, so they work well in large organizations. Capricorns perform best in a team atmosphere and thrive in corporations, unlike Arians, for instance, who are often self-employed. Since Capricorn rules high finance, and because Capricorns understand the value of a chain of command, they often work for powerful, well-established companies. Saturn propels them to high, but perhaps lonely, positions at the top, but Capricorns don't mind the isolation such a position of authority may bring.

Capricorns are successful in banking, insurance, or any field that involves large budgets. Their sense of responsibility and ethics instills trust in those who employ them. This sign values routine and proves the adage "Slow and steady wins the race." As an earth sign, Capricorn bases decisions on facts, not on intuition. These industrious, duty-minded types wouldn't be caught asleep at the wheel. Capricorns eagerly work for the betterment of the whole and do not let their egos dictate their actions. This sense of community inspires them to work as volunteers for charitable organizations, often becoming their leaders.

They do, however, need constant recognition. Money and security may motivate Taureans, but prestige attracts Capricorns. Still, they take their roles as providers seriously. When it comes to money, Capricorns, like Taureans, spend for classic, well-designed, quality items with enduring value—and they often find their purchases at bargain prices!

Capricorn values tradition and family heritage. You can tell a Capricorn bride by the dress she is wearing—Mother's—and the lovely heirloom pearls she has around her neck—Grandmother's. Capricorns happily pay regular visits to relatives who appreciate their good-natured temperaments, and they especially help those in need, because they are generous, patient, and sensitive. Respect for the past and their interest in preserving it may lead them to become archaeologists, historians, or antique dealers. With Saturn's rulership over teeth and bones, Capricorns also make good dentists and orthopedic surgeons.

Capricorns make the best comedians in the zodiac for a very logical reason. As many psychologists point out, people often need to laugh at serious or difficult subjects. Capricorn, ruled by earnest Saturn, meditates on the darker side of life and therefore feels compelled to poke a little fun at it.

If you settle down with a Capricorn, you will have a loyal and steadfast mate who provides well. Your future will be bright and free from financial worry. Change and progress will punctuate your successful life together.

19
Jennifer Beals, actress
Robert Urich, actor
Cicely Tyson, actress

20
Kiefer Sutherland, actor
Irene Dunne, actress
Harvey Firestone, founder of Firestone Tire & Rubber Co.

21
Jane Fonda, actress
Florence Griffith-Joyner, Olympic track athlete
Chris Evert, tennis player

22
Capricorn

Diane Sawyer, TV journalist
"Lady Bird" Johnson, First Lady
Giacomo Puccini, composer

23
Jose Greco, flamenco dancer
Robert Bly, writer
Yousuf Karsh, photographer

24
Ava Gardner, actress
Mary Higgins Clark, writer
Cab Calloway, bandleader and singer

25
Christmas

Clara Barton, founder of the Red Cross
Isaac Newton, mathematician and discoverer of law of gravity
Annie Lennox, singer

26
Carleton Fisk, baseball player
Henry Miller, writer
Steve Allen, comedian and TV host

27
Marlene Dietrich, actress and singer
Gerard Depardieu, actor
Cokie Roberts, TV journalist

28	Denzel Washington, actor Maggie Smith, actress Woodrow Wilson, 28th United States president
29	Ted Danson, actor Mary Tyler Moore, actress Pablo Casals, cellist
30	Rudyard Kipling, writer Tracy Ullman, comic actress Bo Diddley, singer
31 New Year's Eve	Anthony Hopkins, actor Ben Kingsley, actor Henri Matisse, artist

GIFT IDEAS FOR
THE CAPRICORN MAN

*Something from a fine retailer (Capricorn is status conscious) • stocks or bonds
from a company he has researched • rare stamps or coins • a book on a historical subject (Capricorn
rules history) • an old and rare handwritten letter or document • membership to
a natural history museum • a pair of hiking boots*

GIFT IDEAS FOR
THE CAPRICORN WOMAN

*A piece of estate jewelry • your grandmother's heirloom brooch
• your mother's pearls (her sign rules history and antiques) • classic and elegant
clothing in a neutral color • a well-cut tweed jacket in dark green
or gray • a fine designer silk scarf*

	COLORS	GEMS
 **Aquarius** *January 20–February 18*	electric or iridescent blues, fuschia, hot pink, bright turquoise, charcoal gray	aquamarine, amazonite, hematite
Pisces *February 19–March 20*	sea green, silvery white, pale lavender to deep violet, aqua, purplish blues, pale bluish pinks, and other "water" colors	amythyst
Aries *March 21–April 19*	bright red	diamond, ruby
Taurus *April 20–May 20*	pale pink, pale blue, shades of green	emerald
Gemini *May 21–June 20*	pale lemon yellow	agate, alexandrite, tourmaline
Cancer *June 21–July 22*	white, silver, iridescent pale blue, smoky blue, smoky gray	moonstone, pearl
Leo *July 23–August 22*	gold, orange, scarlet, deep purple	ruby, peridot, amber, topaz, yellow diamond
Virgo *August 23–September 22*	dark brown, forest green, gray-green, navy blue	sardonyx, jasper, hematite, jade, carnelian, agate, hyacinth
Libra *September 23–October 22*	dusty pink, pale blue, deep rose, pale green	opal, sapphire
Scorpio *October 23–November 21*	burgundy, maroon, eggplant, black	bloodstone, fire opal, carbuncle, selenite, black pearl
Sagittarius *November 22–December 21*	royal blue, purple	turquoise, lapis lazuli, agate, obsidian
Capricorn *December 22–January 19*	indigo, teal, dark colors, such as chocolate brown, navy blue, gray, and black	garnet, black pearl, black onyx, white sapphire

FLOWERS	TREES	BIRD	SCENTS
wild orchids, wisteria, hydrangea, tulip, sweet alyssum, daffodil, anemones, hyacinth	yucca, crab apple, many fruit trees	scarlet ibis, oriole, hawk, owl	sandalwood, orange blossom, geranium, fruity scents
white orchid, violet, narcissus, water lily, gardenia, white lily	weeping willow, fig trees, trees that grow along the water's edge	pelican, pink flamingo, swan, mockingbird	sarsaparilla, eucalyptus, light florals with notes of lilac or violet, light orientals
American Beauty rose, honeysuckle, musk rose, thistle, clove pink, phlox, all flowers with thorns	dogwood, hemlock, fir, hawthorn, blackthorn, wild olive	cardinal, lark, rooster, cat bird	spicy scents, frankincense, myrrh, ginger, jasmine, lemon, honeysuckle, mint, pine
white and purple lilac, primrose, yellow mountain, pink sweetheart rose, violet, daisy, foxglove, dogrose	white birch, ash, apple, pear, fig, cypress	dove, sparrow, thrushes	sandalwood, musk blends, rose
wild rose, sweet pea, lily of the valley, tuberose, iris, cheiranthus, lavender, myrtle	laurel, mulberry, hazel, linden, chestnut, all nut-bearing trees	parrot, mynabird, jaybird, hummingbird	citron, lilac, lily of the valley, lavender, chypre, vanilla (alone or with musk)
lily, moon flower, lotus, acanthus, field rose, convolvulus, clematis, white flowers such as paper whites, white roses, and gardenias	cottonwood, maple, trees with sap	goose, duck, sea gull	jasmine, rose, gardenia, lemon, lotus, honeysuckle, single-note floral fragrances
peony, morning glory, amaryllis, crown imperial, passion flower, marigold, poppy, celandine, sunflower, golden flowers	walnut, bay, olive, citrus trees	peacock, bird of paradise, golden warbler, egret	sandalwood, orange blossom, juniper, sophisticated orientals
orange blossoms, buttercup, hyacinth, veronica, alkanet, cornflower, yellow archangel, forget-me-nots, small, brightly colored flowers	honey locust, white poplar, aspen, nut-bearing trees	lovebirds, cockatoo, robin	lavender, sandalwood, lilac, lily of the valley, fresh, light scents with floral undertones
large roses, jonquil, lupine, primrose, foxglove, bluebells, all blue flowers	alder, cherry, apple, ash, poplar, balsam, sycamore	turtle dove, nightingale, bluebird, bobolink	fragrances with warm, fruity undertones, or rich, well-balanced floral fragrances
chrysanthemum, fuschia, hollyhock, rhododendron, geranium, honeysuckle, all root vegetables	white cedar, hawthorn, box elder, cactus, blackthorn	phoenix, eagle, heron, falcon	musk, florals with warm undertones
carnations, wild pink, dandelion, sweet william, heather	oak, poplar, silver birch, lime, ash	quail, American firetail	woodsy scents, fresh florals, citrus, imported scents
hibiscus, amaranthus, jasmine, pansy	elm, redwood, yew, pine, holly bushes	raven, wren	patchouli, sandlewood, warm florals, orientals, chypre blends

THE SUN, MOON, AND THE PLANETS AND WHAT EACH GOVERNS IN ASTROLOGY

SUN

The Sun, a star, is the giver of life and strength. It rules a person's ego, self-esteem, creativity, generosity, joy, pride, charisma, and magnanimity. The sun sign signifies the basic personality that the public notices first. In a person's chart, the Sun signifies important males in the horoscope: the father, husband, boyfriend, business partner, or boss. Ruler of Leo.

MOON

The Moon rules a person's emotions, moods, inner thoughts, and domestic conditions. It also governs childbirth, children, and nurturing. The Moon in one's chart indicates true character and personality. In a person's chart, the Moon has rulership over important females in the horoscope: mother, wife, girlfriend, business partner, or boss. The Moon is the earth's satellite. Ruler of Cancer.

VENUS

Love, affection, happiness, parties, pleasant pastimes, favors, the social graces, tact, sharing, compromise, value, money, and gifts all come under the planet Venus. It governs perfume, flowers, foliage, trees, beauty treatments and cosmetics, fashion, jewelry, and beautifying accents for the home. Venus is considered feminine and receptive in nature. Ruler of Taurus and Libra.

MERCURY

Mercury rules intellect and a person's approach to the thought process. Logic, perception, listening, adaptability, alertness, research, and dissemination of information are governed by this planet. Mercury also rules transportation, communication, learning, contracts, telephones, faxes, speech, letters, couriers, postal matters, maps, vehicles, roadways, periodicals, on-line information, advertising, public relations, and sales. Ruler of Gemini and Virgo.

MARS

Mars is pure energy and is called "The Great Activator," ruling all efforts that require concentration and determination. This planet can also rule strife if energy becomes excessive. Mars is considered male and active in nature. The location of Mars in a person's chart shows where effort and attention will be given in that area of life. Governs all sharp objects, fire, and combustion, as well as how sexuality is generally expressed. Ruler of Aries and coruler of Scorpio.

JUPITER

Jupiter is called "The Great Benefactor," the giver of gifts and luck. It rules expansion, opportunity, favor, goals, values, faith, optimism, fortune, financial benefits, philosophy, and religion. Ruler of Sagittarius.

SATURN

Saturn has been called "The Taskmaster" and rules responsibility, concentration, self-worth, tangible results from effort, wisdom, ability to deal with reality, self-confidence, authority, ambitions, self-discipline, experience, tenacity, and practicality. Saturn governs bones and teeth, and foundations of all kinds, from the human skeleton, to the base of a house, or the organizational hierarchy of a company. It also has rulership over history and archaeology, artifacts from the past, and antiques. Ruler of Capricorn.

URANUS

"The Great Awakener," Uranus is the planet of surprise, upheaval, change, innovation, shock, eccentricity, the unexpected, humanism, freedom, originality, independence, brotherhood, universality, and social change. Uranus governs electricity, TV, radio, new technology, the future, astrology, electronic equipment, cyberspace, and science fiction. Ruler of Aquarius.

NEPTUNE

Neptune is the higher octave of Venus, which means that it brings beauty to a higher spiritual level. It has rulership over dreams, illusions, inspiration, all non-verbal communication such as ballet, dance, music, art, poetry, film, and photography. It also rules intuition, instinct, idealism, mysticism, and compassion. From its association with Neptune, god of the seas, this planet also rules liquids, floods, ice, and all bodies of water. This planet has a double edge if care is not taken to avoid its other qualities, which are sometimes called "The Mist." These include confusion, misunderstanding, escapism, or deception. Ruler of Pisces.

PLUTO

Rebirth, regeneration, inner strength, power, obsession, overcoming obstacles, intensity, transformation, compulsion, probing, intimacy, and deep seated, obscure sexual needs all come under Pluto. This planet governs hidden or unseen phenomena, so this planet also governs strategy, covert operations, spy work, roots of plants and trees, and all underground vegetables. Ruler of Scorpio.

THE ELEMENTS:
EARTH, FIRE, AIR, AND WATER
Called the Triplicities by Astrologers

EARTH: TAURUS, VIRGO, AND CAPRICORN

Earth signs have their feet firmly planted on the ground and know what it takes to get things done. They are gifted with the ability to make dreams real and tangible. Talented producers who always get results, they understand deadlines, teamwork, budgets, and power. They love beautiful things and know how to care for them. Earth signs are reserved and don't seek the spotlight. In fact, they prefer to work offstage because they know this is where the real influence frequently lies.

FIRE: ARIES, LEO, AND SAGITTARIUS

Fire signs are creative and love to experiment with new ideas and concepts. Fire signs enjoy being the center of attention, and burn more brightly when they are noticed. They are impulsive, spontaneous, even a bit eccentric. They are warm hearted and like the stimulation of being with others. These signs are enthusiastic, "catching fire" about new ideas and plans. As natural leaders, they don't mind being the first to try new things. They are often the trendsetters for their peers.

AIR: GEMINI, AQUARIUS, AND LIBRA

Air signs are intelligent and love to analyze facts. Curious, playful, and verbal, they are the communicators of the zodiac. They sparkle in a crowd because they bring news and information to others. They are meant to socialize and increase their energy by being with others. Breezy and easygoing, they get along with many types of people. Air signs do not hold grudges and prefer to say what is necessary to "clear the air" before they can move on. They are likely to make friends for life.

WATER: CANCER, SCORPIO, AND PISCES

Water signs are more emotional and are more intuitive than other signs. They even may be psychic. Their sharply honed emotions make them compassionate, caring, and nurturing. Water purifies, cleanses, and also holds mystery. These signs *feel* events around them; they have great ability in reading body language, easily interpreting the true emotions and moods of others. Their giving nature and sensitivity can exhaust their reserves, so they occasionally need solitude to recharge and refresh themselves before reentering the world.

THE QUALITIES:
THE CARDINAL, FIXED, AND MUTABLE SIGNS

Called the Quadruplicies by Astrologers

THE CARDINAL SIGNS:
ARIES, CANCER, LIBRA, AND CAPRICORN

Cardinal signs are the pioneers of the zodiac because the month in which each of these signs falls begins its respective season—spring, summer, fall, or winter. People born under cardinal signs are ambitious and continually think of new ideas. They like change for the sake of change. They are restless and like to start projects, and are also very goal oriented. They make terrific leaders.

THE FIXED SIGNS:
TAURUS, LEO, SCORPIO, AND AQUARIUS

The fixed signs consolidate and make permanent what the cardinal signs began. People born under the fixed signs, which follow the cardinal sign within each season, are determined and are able to concentrate exceedingly well. Basically loners, they have a high level of stability and self-assurance. Their downside is their resistance to make changes. Nevertheless, fixed signs ultimately achieve success through their strong persistence.

THE MUTABLE SIGNS:
GEMINI, VIRGO, SAGITTARIUS, AND PISCES

The mutable signs, which follow the cardinal and fixed signs at the end of each season, prepare for change and transition. They mark the end of the old and the beginning of the new and are the most flexible of the signs. Strong communicators, analytical, and intellectual in nature, these signs excel in social situations. When they are upset, they express their views but never hold a grudge. They are excellent in crisis situations, for they quickly perceive what needs to be done and can adapt themselves especially well. They realize that nothing is more constant than change, and in this lies their ultimate power.

PARTY STYLES

CAPRICORN

Capricorns will choose to have a party in a private club or restaurant with a reputation for quality. Wood paneling and other old-world touches would provide the perfect setting for this sign's celebration. At this party, there will be a mix of business friends and personal acquaintances, for Capricorns do not make a distinction between private life and work. The perfect reason for Capricorns to throw a party is to **congratulate a friend,** or themselves, **for a big promotion** or **new job.** They would also enjoy giving **a roast** to an old college pal.

AQUARIUS

Aquarians will give an informal party and use technology in some way to add to the fun. They might give a **virtual reality party** or **a party in two cities, strung together with a video conference monitor.** This sign always sees that the acoustics for music are outstanding. Guests will range from CEOs to mailroom clerks, for Aquarians are very democratic. They might give a **charity fund-raiser,** since they are so humanitarian. Because this sign enjoys politics, Aquarians would enjoy throwing a party in honor of a local candidate on **Election Day,** or a buffet dinner party to watch the election returns as they are televised.

PISCES

Pisceans adore mystery, imagination, and playing make-believe. What better idea for a Piscean than to give a **costume Halloween** or **Masquerade Ball**! Prizes for the best costumes will be presented. A Pisces party will be lit by candlelight and offer plenty of music for dancing. Pisceans prefer sit-down dinners with guests seated at small tables to encourage intimate conversation. To enchant guests, the flowers at a Pisces affair will be chosen not only for beauty but also for their intoxicating scents.

ARIES

Arians love outdoor parties where everyone can spread out, and they like to provide competitive games and sports for guests. Think of having a picnic, or bonfire on the beach, or a barbecue (Aries rules fire). Aries is the sign of the brave, so Arians might throw a **Fourth of July** party or one for a **new business venture** for themselves or in honor of a friend.

TAURUS

The Taurus party requires candlelight, the finest tableware, many flowers, gourmet food, and good conversation. This sign loves sweets, so Taureans might plan a desserts-only party. Taureans' favorite holiday? **Valentine's Day,** of course! Also, think about throwing a party to celebrate the **onset of spring.**

GEMINI

Since conversation is so vital to Geminis, they'll want to throw a crowded cocktail party where a wide variety of delicious hot and cold hors d'oeuvres can be offered. This sign craves variety and runs on nervous energy. Geminis like to mix young and old, friends and family together. Since Gemini rules travel and education, their best party is a **bon voyage bash** for a friend or a **graduation gala** in honor of a young relative.

CANCER

Cancers prize a warm, cozy atmosphere, so this sign will prefer to give a party at home. For food, Cancers like to offer an abundance of tasty, family recipes rather than "chic" cuisine. Cancers shine brightest with the celebration of holiday traditions, so they should plan to give a big **Christmas or Chanukah dinner,** or a party to celebrate the **arrival of a friend's new baby.**

LEO

Leos love drama and elegance, the more opulent the better: candelabra, chandeliers, and a roaring fireplace. Leos enjoy large parties, so they may rent an estate, small castle, or ballroom. It is likely to be a black-tie dinner where guests sit at one long, grand table, replete with the finest tableware. An abundance of food and wines will be served, and the music will be chosen carefully. The perfect reason for a Leo party? **New Year's Eve,** of course!

VIRGO

Virgo is the sign that rules the harvest, and Virgos prefer classic, healthful foods, with plenty of fresh vegetables and fruits. Virgos prefer sit-down dinners for eight to ten people, where lively and intelligent conversation can be sparked. The perfect occasion for a Virgo is an elegant **Thanksgiving dinner,** the very symbol of fruits of the harvest, the holiday Virgos celebrate best.

LIBRA

Venus-ruled Libra is a very social sign, and Librans love a good party. They will make it gracefully elegant, with plenty of flowers, music (live if possible), and the finest foods and wines. Famous people have a way of turning up at a Libran's bash, because Librans know just about *everyone*. The perfect reason for a Libra party for this partnership-oriented sign is to **toast a friend's engagement or wedding,** or to **celebrate an anniversary,** their own or a friend's.

SCORPIO

Scorpios like small and intimate parties, and since this sign rules secrets, they should plan a nighttime **surprise birthday party** for someone they love. Scorpio is a water sign, so they may plan an intensely private affair on a yacht, or reserve an entire inn or small hotel that offers a romantic view of a lake. The food served will be classic, and for dessert Scorpios are likely to serve something deliciously rich, in chocolate.

SAGITTARIUS

Sagittarians' parties are bound to be big, with many high-level friends present, not only from business, but from academia and religious sectors too. This sign likes informality, so throwing a **Labor Day** party at a large, old farmhouse where guests can come to stay for the weekend would be ideal. If there are dogs, cats, horses, and other animals around, so much the better (Sagittarians adore animals). Spontaneous games and sports are likely to break out on the lawn, and an array of unusual foods from various cultures will be offered.

NOTES